goldfish

guide to care, health and
aquarium maintenance

goldfish

guide to care, health and
aquarium maintenance

Magnet & Steel Ltd

www.magnetsteel.com

Every reasonable care has been taken in the compilation of this publication. The Publisher and Author cannot accept liability for any loss, damage, injury or death resulting from the keeping of goldfish by user(s) of this publication, or from the use of any materials, equipment, methods or information recommended in this publication or from any errors or omissions that may be found in the text of this publication or that may occur at a future date, except as expressly provided by law.

No animals were harmed in the making of this book.

The 'he' pronoun is used throughout this book instead of the rather impersonal 'it', however no gender bias is intended.

Printed and bound in China.

ISBN: 978-1-907337-20-8
ISBN: 1-907337-20-2

Contents

The first goldfish

The Chinese first caught fish from the wild 4,500 years ago, and kept them as a source of food.

The Crucian Carp (Carassius carassius), a small brown-coloured fish, was a frequent sight in the cool, slow-moving freshwater rivers and streams of southern China. The Chinese caught carp from the wild, and then set up their own farms to breed fish and sell them as food. Fish farmers noticed that some fish were brighter in colour, more orange than brown, and they decided to breed from these fish to produce gold-coloured fish.

By the time of the Chinese Sung Dynasty, 1,000 years ago, the goldfish was recognised as a breed in its own right. But goldfish were not for eating. They were kept in beautiful ponds, planted with water lilies. Soon keeping fish was a popular hobby among the Chinese.

The Japanese koi (pictured below) may look like the goldfish, but has in fact descended from a different species of carp and has distinctive whiskers around its mouth.

Fancy goldfish

The Japanese also caught carp from the wild, and they developed their own breed, which is known as Koi. These are much bigger than goldfish, and come in a dazzling array of colours. Today Koi are highly prized all over the world.

In the 14th Century, the Japanese turned their fish-breeding skills to goldfish and they developed spectacular new varieties.

They kept their fancy goldfish in ponds, which were decorated with plants and sculptures. Wooden bridges and stepping stone pathways helped to give a really good view of the fish.

Spreading worldwide

News of fancy goldfish spread outside China and Japan in the 19th Century. Ships loaded with goods from the East sailed to Europe. They carried silks and spices, and interesting plants and animals, including fancy goldfish.

In 1853 the world's first public aquarium opened in London. People were fascinated by the fish from the East and fish-keeping became a new hobby.

The first goldfish were exported to North America and Australia in the late 19th Century and soon goldfish were the most popular pet fish in the world. Indeed they rank among the most popular of all pets, with only dogs, cats and rabbits ahead of them.

Perfect pets

Hundreds of different fish species are kept in aquariums, but the goldfish is an all-time favourite. What is the secret of its success?

There are many reasons why goldfish are perfect pets.

- Goldfish are beautiful to look at.

- They are inexpensive to buy.

- There are lots of different varieties to choose from.

- They can be kept indoors in an aquarium or outdoors in a pond.

- They do not take up very much room.

- They are one of the most hardy of all aquarium fish, and can live for up to 25 years (14 years for the fancy varieties).

- If you suffer from pet allergies, which are caused by having animals with fur in the house, keeping goldfish is the perfect solution.

Good luck

Keeping fish can have a calming effect on people. In the Chinese system of Feng Shui, which helps people to live in harmony with their surroundings, goldfish (known as baby dragons) are highly valued. The Chinese word for goldfish is 'yu' which is the same as the word for success, so keeping goldfish was believed to bring good luck.

Special requirements

While it is true that goldfish are relatively easy to keep, and inexpensive to buy and feed, they have specific needs that must be met in order to thrive and live long healthy lives.

In reality, as a fish owner you are in actual fact a water keeper. A fish tank is an entire universe to your goldfish: it is their world, and you control their living environment. You must perform a partial water change at least once a fortnight in order to prevent the water from becoming toxic and unhygienic for your finned friends. You must ask yourself if you have the time to perform these basic duties. Once you have decided fishkeeping is the right hobby for you, your fish will provide you with years of enjoyment throughout their lives in a well maintained system.

Even though keeping goldfish is comparatively straightforward, do not be tempted to rush into buying them. Like all living creatures goldfish have their own special needs.

They must be:

- Housed in a tank that is the correct size for the number of fish you are keeping.

- Kept in fresh, clean water.

- Fed every day.

- Checked regularly to make sure they are in good health.

- Cleaned out on a routine basis.

- Taken care of when you are on holiday.

Goldfish homes

Goldfish are classed as coldwater fish, which means they can live in cold water without special heating equipment. However, they are just as comfortable in more temperate water conditions.

In fact, goldfish can live in an outdoor pond all year round, but you will need to select the hardy varieties which can survive in cold temperatures.

The goldfish

To look after goldfish, you need to understand how their bodies work.

Brain

Goldfish used to be thought of as the dimwits of the animal kingdom with a memory lasting just 3 seconds. However, it has now been shown that a goldfish can recognise members of its own shoal, and knows when it is feeding time.

Nostrils

Goldfish use their sense of smell to find food. They can also smell chemicals in the water.

Eyes

The eyes bulge out slightly, giving the goldfish good all-round vision, even though it cannot turn its head. Compared to many species of fish, the goldfish has excellent vision and can see a distance of 4.5 metres.

Gills

Goldfish do not have lungs. They use their gills to take in oxygen from the water and get rid of carbon dioxide.

Hearing

In fact goldfish do not have ears as we would recognise them. They have a modified hearing organ located inside its body, called the 'Weberian apparatus' to interpret sound. Goldfish dislike loud noises, and will dart away to find a safe hiding place.

Colour

The distinctive colour of the goldfish is made up from three types of light responsive cells. These cells are called Melanocytes (black), erythrophores (red) and xanthophores (yellow).

The traditional metallic a sheen of the goldfish is due to a reflective material (known as guanine) which is on and under the scales. This allows good reflection of light through the scales.

Dorsal fin

This keeps the goldfish stable in the water. It is missing in some fancy varieties, which makes them poor swimmers.

Lateral line

This is a line of cells which alerts the goldfish to any disturbance in the water. The lateral line is a sensory organ. The lateral line is extremely sensitive and can detect motion, current, pressure, and even sound.

Caudal fin

The caudal or tail fin is used to propel the goldfish through the water. In fancy varieties the tail is split down the middle to form twin tails.

Scales

The body is covered in bony scales that overlap each other from the head towards the tail. This allows for streamlining in the water, so the goldfish can swim more easily.

Pectoral fins

These are located on either side of the goldfish, just behind the gills. They are used for forward and backward propulsion and for stability.

Pelvic fins

These are also on either side of the body, between the pectoral and anal fins. They are used for stability and steering.

Anal fin

There is usually one anal fin on the underside of the body. However, some varieties have a double anal fin.

Vent

This is where the goldfish gets rid of waste.

Goldfish are cold-blooded, which means that their body temperature changes depending on the temperature of the water. They can withstand a large range of temperatures, as long as there are no sudden changes.

Goldfish varieties

There are more than 100 varieties of goldfish, so you are certain to find something that takes your fancy!

Goldfish come in different sizes, shapes, and colours, but some are much easier to look after than others. If you go for the more exotic varieties, you will have to make special plans to suit their needs:

- Single-tail goldfish are tough and hardy. But they can grow quite big and may reach up to 12 inches in length (30 cm).

- Fancy goldfish, which include all the twin-tailed varieties, must be kept in an aquarium. They will not survive in a pond. The temperature should be between 18- 23 Centigrade (64- 73 Fahrenheit). Hardy goldfish can live in temperatures between 10- 24 Centigrade (50- 75 Fahrenheit).

- Some fancy varieties have very fine fins, so you

will have to be careful with rocks and other objects in the tank, as fins can easily be ripped.

- Twin-tailed goldfish and varieties without a dorsal fin do not swim as well as the single-tailed varieties. They will lose out if they have to compete for food. It is better not to mix twin-tailed and singled-tailed varieties.

There are too many varieties to show them all in a book this size, but here are some of the types you are most likely to find in your pet store.

Common goldfish

This is the traditional goldfish, which can be any colour ranging from golden red to pale yellow. It is an ideal choice if you are new to fishkeeping. They will live in an aquarium or a pond. Usually a brilliant orange-red or yellow, though young fish are often darker in colour.

Shubunkin

Beautifully-coloured fish with a blue silver body mottled with black, red, brown, yellow and violet. They have streamlined bodies with well-developed and even fins. Generally, they do not grow as big as common goldfish. It can also live in an aquarium or a pond.

Shubunkins possess nacreous scales (a mix of metallic and transparent scales that are pearly in appearance). The overlapping patches of red, white, blue, grey and black (along with dark speckles), which is known as calico, normally extend to the finnage of shubunkins.

Comet

Slender in body shape, the Comet has a long, single tail fin, which can grow up to twelve inches in length.

The Comet is more active than most other goldfish breeds and can swim very fast over short distances. It will live in an aquarium or a pond. The comet can be distinguished from the common goldfish by its long, single and deeply forked tail fin. Comets with yellow, orange, red, white, and red-and-white colouration are common. They were originally bred in the United States.

Ryukin

A goldfish with a short body, a steeply curved back, and flowing fins. It is very round in shape, and looks like a butterfly from the rear. This is the easiest of the fancy goldfish to keep. The Ryukin goldfish was developed in Japan and comes in a huge variety of colours. It is very graceful in motion, its V-shaped tail and paired anal fins giving it a real elegance.

Veiltail

The tail fin hangs in folds, the anal fin is long and delicate, and the dorsal fin is very tall. Veiltails are slow swimmers and can easily become damaged on sharp objects, but they are graceful and beautiful.

Originally bred in the United States, Veiltail goldfish should have a short and rounded body with a smooth outline. The Veiltail goldfish standard requires the trailing edge of the caudal fin to be free from forking or pointed lobes. The caudal fin should be divided, flowing and at least three-quarters of the body length.

Moor

This goldfish, sometimes called the Black Moor, is jet-black in colour and has the outline of a Veiltail. The Moor goldfish is one of the more rounded or egg-shaped fancy gold fish. The rounded body shape of this beautiful fish is enhanced by large bulbous eyes protruding out on the sides of its head, metallic scales that give it a deep velvety black colour, and long flowing finnage.

Lionhead

The Lionhead goldfish is by far the most popular and well known of the goldfish which lack a dorsal fin. Rather than having the long slender body of the Common goldfish or the Shubunkins, the Lionhead is one of the more rounded or egg-shaped fancy goldfish. It has a double caudal fin and a double anal fin. It is named because of the raspberry-like growth on its head which looks a little like a lion's mane. Attractive, but a poor swimmer.

Fantail

One of the few fancy varieties to thrive in a pond, as it tolerates low temperatures well. It is similar in appearance to the Ryukin, but with a shorter fan-shaped tail and a rounder body.

Oranda

The Oranda was created by crossbreeding the Veiltail with the Lionhead. It has an egg-shaped body with a flowing pair of caudal fins. Like the Lionhead, the Oranda also has a growth or wen on its head that is raspberry like in appearance. Similar in shape to the Lionhead, but it does have a dorsal fin. It comes in a variety of colours including calico, orange, red, blue, chocolate, bronze, white, silver, red-white, red-black, panda-coloured, and tricolour. It can grow to a length of 8 to 12 inches (20- 30 cm).

Bubble Eye

The Bubble Eye is a small variety of fancy goldfish with upward pointing eyes with two large fluid-filled sacs alongside. The bubbles are fragile and the fish should be kept separately from boisterous types, and away from sharp tank décor. This fish lacks a dorsal fin and consequently is a poor swimmer.

Pompon

Named for the two 'cheerleader' pompons that are positioned above each nostril. It comes in a variety of colours. The pompon has a similar body shape and finnage to the Lionhead but instead of supporting a head growth it has nasal outgrowths. The extent of the nasal outgrowths, which are enlargements of the nasal septum, vary in pompon goldfish. In some, the outgrowths hang down past the mouth.

If you plan to keep more than one fancy variety, the best combination is Veiltails, Ryukins and Orandas. Moors and Bubble Eyes can also be kept together.

In the wild

The closest wild relatives of the goldfish are the Crucian and the Gibel, species of carp commonly found in lakes and rivers in many parts of Europe and Asia.

During the winter months they go into semi-hibernation, sinking to the bottom and encasing themselves in mud. Goldfish seem to have inherited this ability to survive with very little water or oxygen.

Wild Crucians and Gibels spawn in the spring and early summer, with an individual female laying as many as 250,000 eggs.

The Gibel may reach around 12 inches (30 cm) in lengths but Crucians can grow to almost double that length and weigh as much as 7 pounds (3 kg).

The aquarium

If you are a first-time fish keeper, the chances are that you will keep your goldfish in an aquarium.

Goldfish must have enough room to swim so they do not feel overcrowded. There must also be sufficient oxygen in the water for the fish to remain healthy. The best plan is to buy the biggest tank you can afford.

Positioning the tank

When a tank is full of water it will be very heavy, so you must have a sturdy table or shelf to put it on. The tank will also need to be near an electrical supply. When you are deciding where to put your aquarium, check out the following:

- The main living room is a great place for your aquarium, as you will have the most chance to enjoy it. Just make sure your goldfish do not get too much attention from family members or from visitors who may tap on the glass and upset the fish.

- The kitchen is not ideal, as cooking and cleaning fumes could be harmful to your fish.

- The bathroom must be ruled out as the temperature changes too much.

- Do not position your aquarium close to a radiator or the temperature of the water will be affected.

- The aquarium should not be in direct sunlight, otherwise you will be overrun with algae, a green plant that grows on the sides of a tank.

The aquaria pictured are suitable for 1 or 2 small goldfish.

How many?

In the wild, small fish swim in shoals, as this makes it harder for a predator to attack them. A single goldfish may be safe in your aquarium, but it will not be happy as it will feel as though it is always in danger. You should always keep more than one goldfish, but be careful not to get too many.

Goldfish hate to be overcrowded, and the water will get very dirty if there are too many fish. As a general rule, you can keep 0.5 cm of fish per litre of water. Allowing less room will result in overcrowding. The best plan is to seek advice when you buy your tank, so you can work out the right number of fish to keep.

Filters

Like all living creatures, goldfish need to get rid of their waste, and unless you get a filter, the fish will be swimming around in their own toilet. A filter breaks down the waste that builds up in the water, and so the fish can live in a clean, healthy tank.

There are different types of filter, which can either be attached to the side of the tank, under the tank as an external filter or lie underneath the gravel surface. All filters are powered by electricity either directly or indirectly, and need to be fitted carefully.

Bright lights

You do not need lighting in your aquarium, but it does look good, particularly in the evening. Many tanks come with a hood that is fitted with a fluorescent light tube, and you can switch on the lighting for 10-12 hours a day. Do not over-use the lighting or you will have problems with algae.

Cat safe

If you have a cat, make sure you buy a cover or 'hood' for your aquarium, or your cat may try its paw at fishing. Even if the cat does not succeed, a paw dipped in the water would be very frightening for your goldfish.

Take care

The filter and lighting are both powered by electricity, so take care when you fit the equipment. A responsible adult should always take charge to switch the lighting on or off, and when the filter needs to be cleaned. It is best to use water removed from the aquarium as the water to clean your filter media as fresh tap water will harm the bacteria that colonise the filter media to make it work.

Keep it clean

If you do not have a filter, you will need to take extra steps to keep aquarium water clean.

- Remove a cup or two of water every couple of days and replace with water that is at room temperature and has been treated with dechlorinator.

- Make a partial water change every week, around 20% using dechlorinated water that has been allowed to reach room temperature.

- Clean all ornaments in the tank once a week, but do not use detergent.

Tank set up

|Tank set up

Once you have your electrical equipment fitted, you can create an environment that looks good and is safe for your goldfish.

Surface material

The bottom of the tank should be covered with gravel. This can be brightly coloured, or natural looking. Wash the gravel in water (no detergent!) before you put it into the tank, and then make a slope going from the back of the tank to the front. If you are fitting an under gravel filter, cover it with 7-10 cm of gravel.

Decoration

You can really go to town when it comes to choosing ornaments for your tank. You may like fairytale castles and deep-sea divers, or you may prefer rocks and natural wood. Goldfish seem to like rocks with caves, which they can swim through.

Before buying your tank decorations, check that the items are suitable for a goldfish aquarium. This is important if you are planning to keep fancy goldfish, as their fins can get damaged on the sharp edges of rocks or ornaments.

Plants

Goldfish are great nibblers. Some fish keepers choose artificial plants for the tank, which will not need replacing. But your aquarium will benefit from having living plants – and the goldfish will enjoy hiding among the plants as well as having an occasional snack!

A number of plants thrive in coldwater tanks. They include the following:

- Vallis (Vallisneria spiralis): An excellent plant for beginners but will get eaten by your fish. Needs good lighting to thrive.

- Egeria densa: A member of the waterweed family, this is an excellent plant for beginners. Needs good lighting and will get eaten by your fish eventually.

- Java fern (Microsorium): A broad-leafed plant that grows from a thick root. Not edible and may suffer at temperatures lower than 15°C.

Plant your tank when it is half-full of water so that you will be able to position your plants without getting soaked!

Filling up

You might have thought that you could just turn on the tap and fill up your tank with water. But it is not as simple as that. A healthy aquarium needs to contain high-quality water. Tap water is OK for us to use, but it is not suitable for fish living in an aquarium:

- It may contain a number of different chemicals such as chlorine and chloramine, which are harmful to fish.

- There may be high levels of nitrates and phosphates in the water, which encourage algae growth.

These problems can be solved by using a chemical dechlorinator, which prepares tap water for use in an aquarium. It is available from most pet and aquatic stores.

Before adding water to the tank, you will need to calculate how much dechlorinator you need to add to the water. When you fill the tank, make a note of the volume of water you add.

Temperature

Do not use hot water from the tap when you are filling your tank as it may contain copper, which is harmful to fish. Instead, pour in cold water. This will rise to room temperature gradually, which will suit most varieties of goldfish.

Be patient

Hang on before you rush off to buy your goldfish! Once you have set up your aquarium, wait for a week before you introduce the fish. This gives time for the water to rise to room temperature, and allows the water to reach the correct chemical balance. This can be checked by using a simple test kit, which is available from all good pet stores. Follow the printed instructions and test the water for pH, ammonia, nitrate and nitrite levels to see if it is suitable for the fish. There are products available from your pet store that will add "good" bacteria to your tank when setting up. They will accelerate the maturation process of the filter and water. As with all additives to your aquarium, ensure that you read the directions and calculate the water volume of your tank so that you add the correct amount.

When you fill your tank, place a small saucer on the gravel surface, then gently pour the water on to it. This will help the water to spread evenly, so the gravel is not disturbed and the ornaments do not fall over.

Understand the nitrogen cycle

Every newly set up aquarium goes through a process of establishing beneficial bacterial colonies. Older aquariums also go through periods during which the bacterial colonies fluctuate. Failure to understand this process is the largest contributing factor to the loss of fish. Learning what it is, and how to deal with critical periods during the nitrogen cycle, will greatly increase your chances of successful fishkeeping.

The waste problem

Unlike nature, an aquarium is a closed environment. All the wastes excreted from the fish, uneaten food, and decaying plants stay inside the tank. If nothing eliminated those wastes, your beautiful aquarium would turn into a cesspool in no time at all.

Actually, for a short period of time, a new aquarium does become a toxic cesspool. The water may look clear, but don't be fooled. It's loaded with toxins. Sounds awful, doesn't it? Fortunately bacteria that are capable of converting wastes to safer by-products begin growing in the tank as soon as fish are added. Unfortunately, there aren't enough bacteria to eliminate all the toxins immediately (as mentioned earlier, there are products available that can assist and accelerate the maturation process), so for a period of several weeks your fish are at risk.

However, you need not lose them. Armed with an understanding of how the nitrogen cycle works and knowing the proper steps to take, you can sail through the break-in cycle with very few problems.

When you are starting a new tank, buy a single goldfish and allow it to settle in for a week or two, before introducing more fish. It is best to wait until the nitrogen cycle is complete before adding more fish.

Stages of the nitrogen cycle

There are three stages of the nitrogen cycle, which present different challenges.

Initial stage

The cycle begins the fish is introduced to the aquarium. It's faeces, urine, as well as any uneaten food, are quickly broken down into either ionised or unionised ammonia. The ionised form, Ammonium (NH4), is present if the pH is below 7, and is not toxic to fish. The unionised form, Ammonia (NH3), is present if the pH is 7 or above, and is highly toxic to fish. Any amount of unionised Ammonia (NH3) is dangerous, however once the levels reach 2 ppm, the fish are in grave danger. Ammonia usually begins rising by the third day after fish have been introduced.

Second stage

During this stage Nitrosomonas bacteria oxidise the ammonia, thus eliminating it. However, the by-product of ammonia oxidation is nitrite, which is also highly toxic to fish.

Nitrite usually begins rising by the end of the first week fish have been introduced.

Third stage

In the last stage of the cycle, Nitrobacter bacteria convert the nitrites into nitrates. Nitrates are not highly toxic to fish in low to moderate levels. Routine partial water changes will keep the nitrate levels within the safe range. Established tanks should be tested for nitrates every few months to ensure that levels are not becoming extremely high. Of course, nitrates are also great for plant growth so a planted aquarium will thrive when the nitrogen cycle has reached this point.

Now that you know what is happening, what should you do? Simple steps such as testing and changing the water will help you manage the nitrogen cycle without losing your fish.

The key to success is testing the water for ammonia and nitrites, and taking action quickly when problems occur. You can buy a testing kit from your local pet store.

Test for ammonia

Begin testing on day three after adding the fish, and continue every day until the ammonia begins to drop. After it begins to fall, continue testing every other day until the ammonia reaches zero. If at any time your fish show signs of distress, such as rapid breathing (gilling), clamped fins, erratic swimming, or hanging at the surface for air, take immediate action to lower the ammonia level.

Test for nitrites

Begin testing one week after adding the fish. Continue testing every second or third day, until it reaches zero. Again, if your fish appeared distressed, test for nitrite. If levels are elevated perform an immediate 25-50% water change and test daily until levels drop.

What not to do!

- Don't add more fish - wait until the cycle is completed.

- Don't change the filter media - the beneficial bacteria are growing there. Don't disturb them until they have become well established. As mentioned earlier, use water removed from the tank when doing a water change to clean your filter media.

- Don't overfeed the fish - when in doubt underfeed your fish. Remember that anything going into the tank will produce waste one way or another.

- Don't try to alter the pH - the beneficial bacteria can be affected by changes in pH. Unless there is a serious problem with the pH, leave it alone during the startup cycle process

The right choice

Check out the signs of a healthy goldfish below:

Eyes

The eyes should be bright and clear.

Dorsal fin

This should be straight, and standing upright as the fish swims.

Body

The body should be well-rounded.

Mouth

The fish should open its mouth, but should not appear to be gulping for air.

Gills

All the gills should be red-coloured, and showing steady movement.

Pelvic fins

These should extend out to the sides.

Vent

There should be no sign of sticky waste, or soreness.

Movement

The fish should swim easily. A fish that wobbles or tilts, or rests on the bottom, could be sickly.

Scales

The scales should be free from spots or bumps, or woolly, fungal patches.

Colour

The colour of the fish should be dense and even.

At last it is time to go and buy your goldfish. There are many varieties to choose from, so take your time and observe the fish. If you are planning to keep more than one variety, ask for advice so you get the right mix. Remember, fancy goldfish are not as hardy as the single-tailed varieties.

Arriving home

The goldfish you choose will be put in a polythene bag full of water for the journey home. Do not pour your fish straight into the tank the minute you arrive home. Goldfish hate shocks, such as a change in temperature. You need to wait until the water in the polythene bag is the same temperature as the tank water.

- Open the top of the bag and leave it floating in the tank.

- After 20 minutes, mix the water in the tank with the water in the bag, to minimise pH shock, leave the fish in the bag a further 5 minutes and then release the fish.

Feeding fish

Fish that live in the wild must find their own food, but aquarium fish rely on you to provide the correct diet. Feed your goldfish twice a day, and give only as much food as they will eat within 2 minutes. A floating feeding ring will keep the food in one place so your fish can find it easily.

Goldfish are hardy fish and are not too fussy about the food they eat. They need carbohydrates and vitamins to help them grow and to fight disease. They also need a small amount of protein so they can build muscle. Fortunately, we do not have to worry about preparing food that has all these nutrients in the correct balance. It comes ready-made.

Dried food

Goldfish food comes in a dried form, and this may be made up of flakes, granules or pellets. There are many different brands available, but it is important that you read the label and make sure you are buying food that is especially for goldfish.

Supplements

Wild or pond-living goldfish will eat large amounts of plant or weed, which is not available to an aquarium fish. In order to give your goldfish this type of food (and to save your aquarium plants), you can provide a slice of cucumber, or hang some freshly washed lettuce inside the tank. Your goldfish will love it.

Frozen food

Pond-living goldfish eat shrimps, aquatic worms, and snails, and aquarium fish will certainly enjoy live food, such as bloodworm, daphnia or brine shrimp but it's very difficult to ensure you do not introduce disease by doing this. Frozen food provides your goldfish with the benefits of live food, without as much risk of introducing disease.

Overfeeding

Don't overfeed your goldfish. They will always be keen to come to the surface when you offer food, but too much food is very bad for them. Goldfish will develop health problems if they eat too much, and leftover food will pollute the water, which could kill the fish.

Holidays

You can buy slow-releasing food, which will last your goldfish for a short period, but ideally someone should keep an eye on your fish while you are away. Problems can arise when a friend looks after your fish if they over feed. Make sure that the person looking after your fish knows how much to feed and when!

Goldfish care

If you keep a close check on your aquarium, you can spot any signs of trouble at an early stage.

When you feed your goldfish, take a few minutes to study your fish to see if they all appear healthy. Check that the filter is operating, and have a quick look to see if any plants have been uprooted.

Testing the water

The water needs to be tested every week to make sure it is suitable for your goldfish. Use a test kit that will indicate if there is too much ammonia, nitrite or nitrate in the water.

Water changes

If the water test shows an incorrect balance, you will need to make a water change. Generally, fishkeepers change some of the water every two weeks so that the tank is clean and healthy. If you change the water regularly, you will only need to remove 10-20 per cent of the water at a time, which is much easier than making a complete change.

The easiest way to change water is to buy a gravel cleaner, which is specially made so that it vacuums the gravel, and sucks water out of the tank at the same time.

Before you start siphoning off the dirty water, you need to prepare a bucket of clean water. This will need to stand for a couple of hours so that it reaches room temperature. You will also need to add the appropriate amount of dechlorinator.

Filter maintenance

Keeping your filter in good working order is one of the most important tasks you can do to keep your aquarium water clean. Follow the manufacturer's guidelines for effective maintenance.

Algae growth

Algae is a fine green growth that grows on the sides of the tank, particularly if the tank is in direct sunlight, or if you leave the lighting on for long periods. Algae is not harmful to goldfish, but it does spoil the look of the aquarium. It can be removed quite easily by using an algae scraper once a week.

Fish
behaviour

Watch out for the signs that tell you how your goldfish are feeling.

Happy goldfish

A contented goldfish will be active in the tank, swimming easily between the plants and rocks, and coming to the surface to feed. Its fins will be free flowing, and it will appear bright and alert.

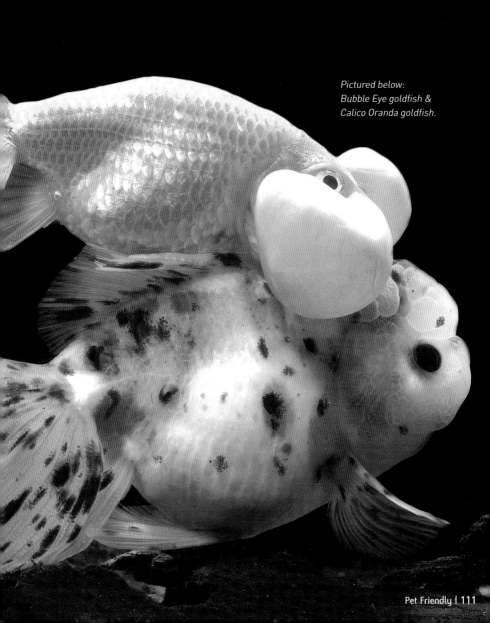

Pictured below:
Bubble Eye goldfish &
Calico Oranda goldfish.

Stressed goldfish

Fish are very sensitive, and they will show signs of stress if their environment is not to their liking. It has been calculated that 90 per cent of problems are down to water quality, so make sure that you test the water regularly.

Other reasons why a goldfish may be feeling stressed include overcrowding, or too few plants in the tank so that there are not enough places for the goldfish to hide.

A stressed fish will:

- Swim with its fins held tight to the body.

- Hang in corners, head down or up.

- Look nervous, as though it is trying to escape.

- Show no interest in food.

- Appear lighter or darker in colour than usual.

Sleeping goldfish

As goldfish have no eyelids, they cannot close their eyes when they sleep. A sleeping goldfish will sink to a low position in the water, usually somewhere out of sight, and will turn a paler colour.

Greetings

When you approach the tank, you may see your goldfish rise to the surface. This is the fish's way of saying hello!

You may see your goldfish tip up, with its head resting on the bottom of the tank and its tail held high. The goldfish has found some food, and its tail is a signal so other goldfish will swim over and enjoy the feast.

Health
problems

Goldfish are hardier than most types of fish, and many health problems are curable if you can get the diagnosis right.

By far the biggest cause of health problems in goldfish is poor water quality – pollution as a result of over feeding, over stocking, poor tap water or faulty equipment – so your first step should always be to test the water.

Test for ammonia and nitrites first, then pH and nitrates. One of the keys to keeping your fish healthy is to check them regularly. The more often you observe them, the more likely you are to spot unusual behaviour or other symptoms.

Signs of ill health

Goldfish are hardier than most types of fish, and many health problems are curable if you can get the diagnosis right.

- Marks on the mouth or lips.

- Eyes that are dull or cloudy.

- Black, red or white marks (other than normal colouring) on the body or fins.

- Scales slightly raised from the body.

- Swimming on the spot.

- Fins held down and close to the body.

- Gasping at the surface.

Skin complaints

Fin/ tail rot & mouth fungus

These are the result of bacterial infection, usually caused by poor water quality. White marks on the edges of the fins and mouth are followed by a reddening of the area and, eventually, rotting away.

Sores and ulcers

These may be caused by bacteria or a viral infection, sometimes on the site of an old wound. They can often be cured by adding an off the shelf remedy from the pet store to the water, though if a virus is involved the condition may recur as the fish's immune system is weakened. In extreme cases, your veterinary will prescribe an antibiotic to add to the water.

Cuts and grazes

These most commonly occur when fish are chasing, or being chased, at high speed. For this reason you need to be careful that any décor you add to your tank does not have sharp edges.

Dead skin and scales resulting from a graze will turn white and if you spot this you should treat the water with an off the shelf remedy. As above, extreme cases may need an antibiotic from your veterinary.

Fungal infections

These often develop on a wound, feeding on the damaged skin or scales. They will appear as white growths on the skin, often looking like strands or clumps of cotton wool (cotton). They are relatively easy to cure.

Parasitic infections

Whitespot

Whitespot is a parasite that burrows under a goldfish's skin, forming white pin-headed cysts. It can also cause gill irritation, which may leave your fish gasping at the surface.

It is simple to cure with a chemical treatment, but it is necessary to treat the whole of the aquarium or pond rather than individual fish.

Fish lice

The fish louse attaches itself to your goldfish's body and sucks juices from it. Flat and scale-like in appearance. The fish louse is a large parasite and it is quite easy to spot. They don't respond well to antiparasitic treatments and are best removed individually if possible. They can be hard to control in ponds because the egg stage is resistant to most chemicals.

Leeches

These are more of a problem in ponds than in the aquarium. They are thin worm-like creatures, that fix themselves to the skin and suck nourishment from the fish.

They are almost impossible to eradicate completely from a pond, though a chemical treatment from your pet or aquatic store will keep them under control.

Other conditions

Dropsy

This is a very distressing condition which causes the Goldfish to swell, making the scales lift and giving the appearance of a pine cone. It may also cause the eyes to swell.

The most common cause is old age, as the organs of the elderly fish tend to be less efficient and lead to the goldfish effectively taking on water. Bacterial and viral infection and poor nutrition are other causes.

Antibiotics may be effective in young fish, but the condition is difficult to treat and often leads to damage to internal organs, resulting in death.

Buoyancy problems

These are most common in fancy varieties with their strangely-shaped bodies.

This may result in pressure building up in the swim bladder – an internal organ filled with gas which determines the height at which the fish swims in the water.

In some fancy goldfish, the swimbladder cannot expand or assume its normal shape which in turn alters the 'centre of gravity/ buoyancy' of the fish.

Trapped gas in the digestive system, again exacerbated by an odd-shaped body, may also be to blame.

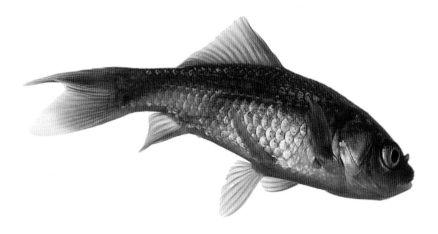

Weights & measures

If you prefer your units in pounds and inches, you can use this conversion chart:

Length in inches	Length in cm	Weight in kg	Weight in lb
1	2.5	0.5	1.1
2	5.1	0.7	1.5
3	7.6	1	2.2
4	10.2	1.5	3.3
5	12.7	2	4.4
8	20.3	3	6.6
10	25.4	4	8.8
15	38.1	5	11

Measurements rounded to 1 decimal place.